NEGATIVE SPACE

Luljeta Lleshanaku was born in Elbasan, Albania in 1968. Under Enver Hoxha's Stalinist dictatorship, she grew up under house arrest. Lleshanaku was not permitted to attend college or publish her poetry until the weakening and eventual collapse of the regime in the early 1990s. She was eventually able to study Albanian philology and literature at the University of Tirana, and later attended the MFA Program at Warren Wilson College, USA. She has worked as a school teacher, literary magazine editor, screenwriter, television author and currently as a research director at the Institute of Studies of Communist Genocide in Albania. She was a fellow of the International Writing Program at the University of Iowa in 1999, and received a fellowship from Black Mountain Institute at the University of Nevada, Las Vegas, 2008-09.

Bloodaxe published her first UK edition, *Haywire: New & Selected Poems*, a Poetry Book Society Recommended Translation, in 2011, drawing on two editions published in the US by New Directions, *Fresco: Selected Poems* (2002) and *Child of Nature* (2010), as well as a selection of newer work, and it was shortlisted for the Corneliu M. Popescu Prize for poetry translated from a European language into English. A new selection, *Negative Space*, was published by Bloodaxe in the UK and *New Directions* in the US in 2018, drawing on two recent collections published in Albania, *Almost Yesterday* (2012) and *Homo Antarcticus* (2015).

She has won several prestigious awards for her poetry, including PEN Albania 2016 (from Albanian PEN Center), National Prize 'Silver Pen, 2000' for poetry, and the International Kristal Vilenica Prize (International Festival of Literature, Slovenia 2009). She was one of the winners of Prishtina Book Fair, 2013 (Kosovo); the winner of KULT Prize, 2013 in Albania for the best book of the year and was awarded 'Author of the Year' by the Publishers Association of Tirana Book Fair, 2013. Her second American collection, *Child of Nature*, was one of 2011 BTBA (Best Translated Book Award) poetry finalists. In 2012 she was one of two finalists in Poland for their European Poet of Freedom prize.

Luljeta Lleshanaku

NEGATIVE SPACE

Translated from the Albanian by
ANI GJIKA

BLOODAXE BOOKS

ISBN: 978 1 78037 412 3

First published 2018 in the UK by
Bloodaxe Books Ltd,
Eastburn,
South Park,
Hexham,
Northumberland NE46 1BS,
and in the US by New Directions Publishing.

www.bloodaxebooks.com
For further information about Bloodaxe titles
please visit our website or write to
the above address for a catalogue.

Supported using public funding by
**ARTS COUNCIL
ENGLAND**

ENGLISH
PEN

FREEDOM
TO **WRITE**
FREEDOM
TO **READ**

This book has been selected to receive financial assistance from English PEN's Writers
in Translation programme supported by Bloomberg and Arts Council England. English
PEN exists to promote literature and its understanding, uphold writers' freedoms around
the world, campaign against the persecution and imprisonment of writers for stating their
views, and promote the friendly co-operation of writers and free exchange of ideas.

Cover design: Neil Astley & Pamela Robertson-Pearce.

Printed in Great Britain by Bell & Bain Limited, Glasgow, Scotland, on
acid-free paper sourced from mills with FSC chain of custody certification.

The true mystery of the world is the visible, not the invisible.

OSCAR WILDE

ACKNOWLEDGEMENTS

This edition presents a selection of poems by Luljeta Lleshanaku published in Tirana by Shtëpia e Librit OMBRA GVG: *Pothuajse Dje* (Almost Yesterday, 2012) and *Homo Antarcticus* (Homo Antarcticus, 2015)

This book has been selected to receive financial assistance from English PEN's Writers in Translation programme supported by Bloomberg and Arts Council England. English PEN exists to promote literature and its understanding, uphold writers' freedoms around the world, campaign against the persecution and imprisonment of writers for stating their views, and promote the friendly co-operation of writers and free exchange of ideas.

Each year, a dedicated committee of professionals selects books that are translated into English from a wide variety of foreign languages. We award grants to UK publishers to help translate, promote, market and champion these titles. Our aim is to celebrate books of outstanding literary quality, which have a clear link to the PEN charter and promote free speech and intercultural understanding.

In 2011, Writers in Translation's outstanding work and contribution to diversity in the UK literary scene was recognised by Arts Council England. English PEN was awarded a threefold increase in funding to develop its support for world writing in translation. www.englishpen.org

CONTENTS

from **Homo Antarcticus** (2015)

FROM

Almost Yesterday

(2012)

Almost Yesterday

Strangers are building a new house next door.
They shout, swear, cheer.
Hammers and a bustle of arms.
They whistle melodies
bookended by hiccups.

Their large window opens to the east.
A lazy boy in sandals
drags a bucket of water half his size.
Sedative.
The world holds its breath for one moment.
The page turns.

Trucks loaded with cement
leave the symbol for infinity in the dirt.

Along the wall, a plumb line measures the height
like a medallion hanging into space
or from someone's neck whose face
nobody bothers to look at.

They started with the barn.
This is how a new life begins –
with an axiom.

I remember my father
returning sweaty from the fields
at lunch break; he and mother
coming out of the barn
tidying their tangled hair in a hurry,
both flushed, looking around in fear
like two thieves.

Their bedroom was cool and clean
on the first floor of the house.

I still ask myself: 'Why in the barn?'
But I also remember
that the harvest was short that year,
the livestock hungry;
we were on a budget
and switched the lights off early.

I was twelve.
My sleep deep, my curiosity numbed,
tossed carelessly to the side
like mounds of snow along the road.

But I remember the barn clearly, as if it were yesterday,
almost yesterday.
You cannot easily forget what you watch with one eye closed,
the death of the hero in the film,
or your first eclipse of the sun.

Small-town Stations

Trains approach them like ghosts,
the way a husband returning after midnight
slips under the covers,
keeping his cold feet at a distance.

A post office. A ticket booth. The slow clock hanging from a nail.
Some of the passengers have been sitting in the same chairs for a
    while now.
They know that you must wait for the moment
and that the moment will not wait for you.

Only a few get on; fewer get off.
The man sitting on a bench
kills time reading a local newspaper.

Train platforms are all the same,
except for the boy hiding behind the pole,
the collar of his school uniform askew.
He is not the firstborn, but the prodigal son,
the chosen one for adventure and the parable of return.

Fried dough, candy, mint sodas ... !
It's the wandering vendor who stirs the thick air
with his clumsy voice.
His pockets are empty but deep.
Dust clings freely
on his sticky fingers, along with a strand of hair,
and in the evening, sometimes,
an entire city.

You don't forget small-town stations easily,
the short stops with ordinary charm.

If you pay attention to every detail,
they will become our alibi for not arriving on time
or for never arriving at all
wherever we had set out to go.

The Unknown

When a child is born, we name it after an ancestor,
and so the recycling continues. Not out of nostalgia,
but from our fear of the unknown.

With a suitcase full of clothes, a few icons, a knife with a shiny blade,
the immigrant brought along names of places he came from
and the places he claimed he named New Jersey, New Mexico,
        Jericho,
New York and Manchester.

The same condition for the unknown above us:
we named planets and stars after capricious, vengeful gods –
Mars, Jupiter, Saturn, Venus, Centaur –
as if making a shield against the cosmos.

Names leap ahead like hunting hounds,
with the belief they clear the road
of the journey's unexpected obstructions.
And we call 'destiny' our common unknown,
a genderless, unconjugated, unspecified name.
Its authority hangs on one shoulder
like the tunic of a Roman senator
leaving only one arm bare and free.

History Class

The desks in the front row were always empty.
I never understood why.
The second row was all smacking lips
of those who recited the lessons by heart.

In the middle were the timid ones
who took notes and stole the occasional piece of chalk.
And in the last row, young boys craning their heads
towards the beauty marks on the blonde girls' necks.

I don't remember the teacher's name, the room,
or the names of the portraits on the wall,
except the irony clinging to the stump of his arm
like foam around the Cape of Good Hope.

When his healthy arm pointed out Bismarck,
his hollow sleeve gestured in an unknown direction.
We couldn't tell which one of us was the target,
making us question
the tiniest bit of who we thought we were.

Out of his insatiable mouth flew battle dates,
names, causes. Never resolutions or winners.
We could hardly wait for the bell
to write our own history,
as we already knew everything in those days.

But sometimes his hollow sleeve
felt warm and human, like a cricket-filled summer night.
It hovered, waiting to land somewhere. On a valley or roof.
It searched for a hero among us –
not among the athletic or sparkly-eyed ones,
but among those stamped with innocence.

One day, each one of us will be that teacher
standing before a seventeen-year-old boy
or a girl with a beauty mark on her neck.
And the desks in the front row will remain empty,
abandoned by those who are always in doubt.
They're the missing arm of history
that makes the other arm appear omnipotent.

Children of Morality

It was the Europeans who taught indigenous people shame,
beginning with the covering up of intimate parts.

Other civilisations were luckier.
Morality was handed to them ready-made from above,
inscribed on stone tablets.

Where I grew up, morality had a form, body, and name:
Cain, unremorseful Mary Magdalene, Ruth, Delilah and Rachel.

Morality was easily pointed at by a seven-year-old's ink-stained
    finger.
Perfect examples of vice or virtue
where time lays its eggs on a swamp.

And so I received the first lessons in morality
without chewing them like cough syrup;
other things happened more abstractly
and under a chaste roof.

And strangely, even the second generation didn't disappoint:
their descendants became another Cain, another Ruth,
another Mary Magdalene who never grew up.
Clichés were simultaneously risky and protective for them,
like trying to use dry snow to make an igloo.

Now I know so much more about morality.
In fact, I actually could be a moralist,
pointing my index finger out as a rhetorical gesture.
But without referring to anyone. Where did everyone go?

A door opened by accident.
Light broke through by force
and, as in a dark room,
erased their silver bromide portraits
which were once flesh and bone.

Night Fishing

He attends funerals. It's his latest hobby.
Nobody knows who he is
or what connects him to the dead person.
They shake his hand without asking questions
(this isn't a wedding
where you must have an invitation).

He doesn't know the dead man's name,
if he'd been young or old, short or tall,
what his job was, if he left any debts, and especially if,
for him, death was an end or a beginning.

(And why should he know this anyway?)

He follows the row of backs turning towards the exit,
their accidental brush
against the marble angels' welcoming wings.

Names, dates are whispered,
and *koliva* trembles in paper cups.
Headstones mark burial plots
already reserved –
clean and proud
like blank cheques.

                    *   *   *

When he was a child,
he eavesdropped on a fisherman
returning to the dock at midnight,
his boat filled with bass he had sold
before catching them.

19

Crabs are an easy lure for bass at night
and bass for the fisherman
and the fisherman for the shore
drawn to an artificial fly at the end of the line.

Even the shore itself is a lure
for the dark waters, high tides under a full moon,
apotheosis of the universe.

*   *   *

'Suddenly, today, he got up before dawn.
Didn't have any pain anymore. Asked for something to eat.
At that moment it hit us that he would be gone.'

'What did he ask for?'

'Leftovers from dinner.'

'Do you think he understood?'

'What we don't know makes us appreciate what little we have.'

'Perhaps... do you know what happens to those on death row?
I heard they can choose their last meal themselves
before being tied to the electric chair.'

'You don't say!'

*   *   *

What is the difference between these people
hurrying towards the exit of the graveyard
and the ten brothers, Jacob's sons, who threw Joseph into a pit,
in the heart of the desert, leaving him
at the mercy of the first merchant to pass by?

In any case, the living cannot wait to leave and turn away.
Their backs a single starless fabric
like fishing nights,
or like a low cloud of gunpowder
in a temporary ceasefire zone.

koliva: boiled wheat used liturgically, mainly at funerals, in Eastern Orthodox
Churches.

Tobacco

Here, everyone smokes.
In the evening, every wife
recognises her respective husband
by the faraway glow of his cigarette
at the end of a cobblestone street.

When the pulse of the glow increases, the wives
feel the storm rushing in and hurry to the fire to cook dinner.
But when the glow is scarce and lazy
like the dying fluorescence of a jellyfish on the sand,
they know they should be quiet and leave the men alone.

At the café
where three people smoke around a table
the fourth cannot refuse a cigarette.
(You cannot stand outside a Shamanic fire,
where despair
is offered with a hand over the heart.)

When they talk about women,
the ash of the half-burned cigarette
hangs expectantly
and a thick yellow ribbon of smoke
encircles them like the police tape
at the scene of a crime.

Later, one husband
starts to share how he has just punished his son
by sending him into the mountains with the sheep for two weeks.
Then he goes quiet. His hands dig into his pockets
as he waits for approval, but he only gets tobacco crumbs.

A cigarette.
There's always a man behind it,
a man once a shepherd who detested his own father
and now savours the solemnity
of being hated in return.

My uncle, too, smokes non-stop.
His ashtray is a navel
stuffed with the fibres of each day
ageing on his body.

Outside in the yard
rain and snow make haste
to wipe out whatever discarded cigarette butts
as though they were spent shells
from a civil war devoid of glory.

Second-hand Books

On one of those mornings
when all the clocks' hands point to the nadir
and greying snow neutralises heartburn,
the only sound is the ringing of the doorbell:
a book ordered weeks ago left on the front steps.
The postman doesn't need confirmation.

Geography III, a second-hand book by Elizabeth Bishop.
Packaged carefully. The address clearly printed on the box
and the portrait of a stern politician on three stamps.

A previous owner
has marked several lines, placing
his own geography next to her words:
'...my poor old island's still
un-rediscovered, un-renameable.
None of the books has ever got it right.'

Who was this reader? A man or woman?
Maybe lying in bed, without anyone around,
heavily underlining, several places in red,
or commenting in blue while
waiting at an airport for a delayed flight.
But the loops that circle words are isobars –
one needs to have reached rock-bottom to understand these marks.

And now it's my turn to add my own geography.
There's hardly any space left, not even for shadows.
The black ring of a coffee cup and the careless ash of a cigarette
are my only traces. My fear of clarity.

A future reader might be my daughter (or one of my nieces)
who could prefer darkness and the scent of pencil lead.
She's left to dog-ear the pages, tear the corners with her lips,
and unknowingly a blonde strand of hair drops onto the page.

And yet another reader
will not leave any traces at all
but simply sell the book to a map collector
and thus create their own geography,
their own religion.

Indeed none of us will read it to the end,
running away from it abruptly the way one evacuates a house,
leaving everything suspended:
the cat scratching the cabinets for food, an abandoned shoe,
the tap's thin trickle, beds still warm,
the TV screen broadcasting a regularly scheduled film,
and time which needs an audience to exist.

Negative Space

I was born on a Tuesday in April.
I didn't cry. Not because I was stunned. I wasn't even mad.
I was the lucky egg, trained for gratitude
inside the belly for nine months straight.
Two workers welded bunk beds at the end
of the delivery room. One on top of the other.
My universe might have been the whitelime ceiling,
or the embodiment of Einstein's bent space
in the aluminium springs of the bed above
that curved towards the centre.

Neither cold, nor warm.
'It was a clear day,' my mother told me.

It's hard to believe
there were a few romantic evenings
when I was conceived, a buzz in the retina
and red-laced magma
decadently peeling off
a silver candlestick.
Infants' cries and milk fever
turned to salt from the stench of bleach –
abrasive, unequivocal.
With a piece of cloth wrapped on the end of a stick,
the janitor casually extends the negative space
of the black-and-white tiled floor
like a mouth of broken teeth, a baleen of darkness
sieving out new human destinies.

2

1968. At the dock, ships arriving from the East
dumped punctured rice bags, mice
and the delirium of the Cultural Revolution.
A couple of men in uniform
cleared out the church
in the middle of the night.
The locals saw the priest in the yard
wearing only his underwear, shivering from the cold.
Their eyes, disillusioned, questioned one another:
'Wasn't he the one who pardoned our sins?'

Icons burned in front of their eyes,
icons and the holy scriptures.
Witnesses stepped farther back,
as if looking at love letters
nobody dared to claim.

Crosses were plucked from graves. And from each mouth
spilled irreversible promises:
mounds of dirt the rains would smooth down
sooner or later.

Children dragged church bells by the tongue.
(Why didn't they think of this before?)
Overnight, the dome was demolished, instantly revealing
a myriad of nameless stars that chased the crowd
like flies on a dead horse.

And what could replace Sunday mass now?
Women brought cauldrons into the yard.
Men filled up their pipes; smoke rose
into the air, against gravity's pull.
Nails in worn out shoes exposed stigmata
that bled in the wrong places –

a new code of sanctification,
of man, by man.

3

'Read!' – I was told. Who said that?
Angel Gabriel, or my first grade teacher
who had dark roots underneath her bleached curls?

Language arrived fragmentary
split in syllables, spasmodic
like code in times of war.

'Continue where your classmate left off!'
A long sentence tied us to one another
without connotation as if inside an idiom.
Someone would get to read the noun, another the verb,
a third one a pronoun...
I always got the exclamation mark at the end –
a mere grimace, a small curse.

A tall cast-iron stove below the portrait of the dictator,
puffing smoke from its temples, enough heat for everyone.
On the blackboard,
leftover diphthongs from yesterday or the day before
rubbed against one another like kittens.

After dusk, I looked for another language outside the window,
my eyes glued to a constellation
(they call these types 'dreamers')
my discovery possibly a journey into the past,
towards a galaxy already dead, non-existent,
the kind of news that needs millions of years
to reach me.

'Read!' – the angel shook me for a third time
her finger pointing to an arbitrary word
a million light years apart from its object. (It didn't matter who
      was first.)
Negative space sketched my onomatopoeic profile
of body and shadow in an accidental encounter.

      4

Language is erosive.
It makes us recluses,
a wind through the canyons
carving our palaeontological eras
for everyone to read.

Under the revised testament of my skin
bellows a gold-cast bull, an alluring object,
a need for attention.
Then comes the unleavened bread and a last supper,
which, remarkably, is repeated several times
between ice ages.
Lower yet, Sodom.
I recognise it from the stench of sulphur.
I hold my nose. Freud would have done the same.
And then Cain,
a crow taught him how to bury his own brother...
And at the bottom,
Adam's gentlemanlike sin
under which scientists
discover earlier epochs of famine.

Between unidentified layers,
wanderings in the sand, the search for a new prophet...

I try to understand my people.

Their language is plain. Some words,
were actually never uttered, like pages stuck together
in a book fresh off the press
and long after it sits on a shelf.

This, too, lives inside me
within insidious bubbles of air, negative
spaces where I can find little historical rest,
but also where utter ruin may originate.

5

Little left of the snow three days ago.
Its blanket ripped away, exposing
dog shit and the bruises of routine.

Negative space gives form to the woods
and to the mad woman – a silhouette
of the goddess Athena
wearing a pair of flipflops,
an owl on her shoulder.

It's minus zero. The factory's gate gnashes its teeth
behind the back of the last worker. Blowing noses, shivering,
        mucus...
A virus circulates through the workplace,
secretly, intimately touching one person after another,
a current of sensuality.
It softens the tone.

But nothing unites them more than their frailty,
the one-size-fits-all shoes you must grow accustomed to
by filling the extra space with cotton,
or curling your ill-fitting toes.

6

In Halil's yard
rules were sacrilege.
His eight children entertained themselves
by carrying famine on their shoulders,
recalling St Bartholomew's flayed skin.
Starving, filthy, hazel-eyed –
three qualities that unexpectedly coalesce
in the bright light, strung together like sneezes.

One's famine was another's consolation.
'Look at them! It's a sin for us to complain.
They're worse off than us!'
But even Halil found his own consolation
in the old woman Zyra, 'barren and paralysed',
the root origin of despair.

This was our highlands landscape,
hierarchical, where each family
would make out a different expiration date
on the roof below their own.

Schadenfreude was the only river
that could turn mills.

But if this hierarchy shifted,
and our roof gave signs of ruin,
my mother would plant tulips in the garden,
white tulips, our false image,
a scarecrow to keep predators away.

7

Nearly nothing was mentioned in the letters he sent from prison,
just two lines, on top of the page:
'I am well...' and 'If you can,
please send me a pair of woollen socks.'

From them, I learned to read between the lines:
negative spaces, the unsaid, gestures,
insomnia that like a hat's shadow
fails to shade your chin and ears.

And in the photographs' white background,
acrophobia adds to the colour of their eyes: blue,
green, grey, and ultimately, chestnut brown,
as, earthward, we lower our gaze.

I learned to read the empty spaces the dead left
behind – a pair of folded glasses
after the reading's done and discourse commences.

Or the musical chairs game called 'love',
where there are less empty seats than people.
If you don't want to be the last one standing
you must predict when the music will stop.
(Who, though, has really succeeded?)

Perhaps a little practice can be useful in this case.
I don't mean squatting, jumping, stretching,
but listening to the same music every day from the start,
the same miserable vinyl record
so that you'll recognise its cracks
before it recognises yours.

8

Midnight. Snoring,
meaningless sounds that stain the side of the wall
that belongs to no one.
So where are we? What dimension?
Who foots the bill at a time like this
without lambs or sinners,
when even angels record nothing?

The street's clearly visible
under the neon 24-hour-service sign
above the funeral home.
There was a music shop next to it
that closed down a few months ago;
the shop shared a wall with the funeral home,
shared the same water pipes and the same gate to heaven.
But the coffins won,
the wide-shouldered coffins that narrow down
in the shape of a mummy, not a human.
Wood of the highest quality, swears the owner,
and pure silk inside, pleated like a stomach
that can digest even a bulldozer.

When asleep we're simply five limbs. Starfish.
If you cut one limb, it will grow back.
Even a single limb could recreate us from the beginning,
a single hope.
Negative space is always fertile.

9

No one knows if it was simply a matter of mixed genes
or some other reason why I used to see
what I wasn't supposed to see –
the ending of things.

It wasn't a mystical gift, but like a blood clot
in the darkness of a vein, I held on to reason,
as it circulated from the bottom up
and not the other way around as we were told.
I used to start from the edges
and with my left hand or a croupier's stick
gather the balls and dice from the corners
and then watch the bettors
as neither a winner nor a loser.
There's nothing sillier
than watching a film in reverse
where after the climax, the protagonists
are replaced by circumstances,
and circumstances replaced by minor characters,
their tongues plastered behind a single, fatal smirk.
Life and my short lunar calendar slipped away
like carbon paper sending off as much light as necessary,
skipping the details, the contrast and sharp colours.
Lunar time is short. Until the actual end,
there are years enough, the negative spaces.
What to do with them when the verb
has already been uttered, a conclusive sentence
with Latin syntax, or more than that:
didactic.

Mine, Yours

One of the few things my mother saved was a doll.
It was the same height as my six-year-old self,
with the same grey-coloured eyes, brown hair,
the same fear of the dark
and drawn to it.
'Don't touch her!' I was told.
'I have nothing else to sell if we go broke!'
Until the day I secretly stole her
and broke her heel by accident.
It was worth nothing now. No capital.
And then it became mine.

I met you one day in May –
pure blue sky with sparse white clouds on the horizon
and nothing more, as if tiny drawings on a biscuit box
made to look tasty to angels and not humans.
What could I do to own such a day
except give it a hard kick in the heel?

For Achilles, the heel would be meaningless
if he hadn't had to choose between glory and a happy life.
Happiness is anonymous, a face without features.
It belongs to no one. But glory, yes. Even to this day
he drags it behind him – his one and only divine defect.

And the motherland? If there weren't a cracked pane
of glass between us, an ethereal wound, an undeniable
physical reality no matter the side that bleeds,
I would doubt such a place even exists.

We do everything we can to own life –
'my life', 'your life' –
when in fact, the opposite happens.
Life needs more than a heel to fasten you to itself;
it hits you hard on the neck
and splits you in two, with no time for wonder.
So one day, you find yourself
exhibited in two separate museums at once.

At this very moment, I cannot be sure
which part of me is speaking to you
and which part the guide's
commenting on and pointing to.

The End of Summer

The summer is coming to an end.

I don't mean the emptied swimming pools,
nor the wind digging in the sand
for carcasses, like a coyote pup.

I am referring to another summer
and other signs.

The moment you feel your star cooling off
and so you pull it out of your chest
and stitch it on your jacket like a badge,
or on the collar of your coat
so that others may finally notice it.

The moment you learn how to negotiate –
five desserts for a single cigarette,
five years of life for a failed romance,
five butterfly lives for five caterpillar days in a cocoon –
you understand
that bitterness is the key to existence.

And when you notice the landscape of your mother's face
and your father's gestures are repeated perfectly in you
without a single alternative, like a city settling into routine
after the decorations from a euphoric celebration are taken down.

What happened to that which once made us unique?

Unknown hands slip
promotional leaflets under the door
with offers of end-of-season clothes.

Summer's stock.

And under the pillow at night,
other hands secretly slip incentives
priced at 50% off, which half of our pride
will continue to turn down
for a little while longer...

Via Politica

I grew up in a big house
where weakness and expressions of joy
deserved punishment.
And I was raised on the *via politica*
with the grease of yesterday's glories,
a thick grease collected under arctic skies.
I was lit up. My notebooks, my hair, my heart reeked of smoke.

That's when we saw each other clearly.
Or rather, what remained of us.
Damaged like lottery numbers
scratched away with a blade.

How different we were!

Those with round faces were righteous;
those with narrow faces were cautious.

One listened secretly to Puccini,
another to silence, the music's music.
The oldest one declaimed monologues
inside a ten by ten foot cell
he had built for himself.

And the mysterious ones
simply had diabetes.

But how similar we were in severe circumstances!
Alarmed like a flock of magpies
that the smallest stone sends into the sky
towards the mouth of the abyss.

Then it became obvious there wasn't enough space for everyone.
We separated. Some went on living *via verbum*,
telling of what they knew, what they witnessed,
and so, through their narrative,
creating their own grease.

The others crossed over the ocean.

And those in particular who went furthest away
never speak of their annoying history
of wretched survival, burying it
in the darkest crevices of their being.
Unfortunately, as with perfume, its scent
lingers there for much, much longer.

The Deal

Nothing ever stays the same.
The acacia and fig tree chopped down.
Under the shade of the fig leaves,
a baby Buddha used to soothe his stomach,
not his mind.

The furniture's gone. So are the letters from prison.
The double-pleated jacket was the last to be thrown out,
the one with dozens of buttons, reeking of naphthalene,
a relic of the 40s.

The same dose of oestrogen
has smoothed burdens from people's faces,
and the balcony that had been hit by a cannonball
has now grown a double chin.

In the evening, the Imam calls to prayer.
This, too, never happened before. Back then,
people used instinct when choosing
between good and evil, heaven and hell,
if they existed.

'I've come to write,' I explain.
'Is that so? And what do you speak of in your writing?'
asks my uncle, sceptically.

He's able to distinguish between 'speak' and 'write',
between a psalm and a sigh.

His voice blends with the one from the TV,
like a heart that beats with the rhythm of a pacemaker
implanted on the other side of the chest.

Only my eyes haven't aged, the eyes of witness,
useless now that peace has been dealt.

In the Town of Apples

The shadow of a pregnant woman –
a soft row of hills in mid-June.

For several months,
she kept her pregnancy hidden,
the same way the children of the exodus
hid their favourite toys
among woolen sweaters and loaves of bread
when told to take only the clothes on their backs.

A gypsy and his little boy
arrive from nowhere
and stop at her feet.
In his hands
an accordion spreads its wings
like an eagle over its prey,
exposing its white, puffed up chest.

An apple is placed on the boy's head
as on the head of every boy in town –
half-rotten apples await a paternity test.

And the fathers
lose their strength
long before shooting the arrow.
Everyone grows old at the same time,
clipped by the same gardener's hand.
The middle generation does not exist.
They migrate,
and when they return,
they have grey hair and build a big grey house
where they'll breathe their last.

But winter is always a good time for apple trees.
Apples everywhere – apples have no memory
and yet, as in Genesis,
they keep playing the temptation game
here, where there is no paradise to lose.

Indifferent wives open windows
and let the nights escape
as if unleashing dogs
on a street that stinks of rotting apples
or maybe cedars.

Acupuncture

Among the personal objects inside a 2100-year-old Chinese tomb,
archaeologists found nine acupuncture needles,
four gold and five silver.
Long before knowing why,
ancient doctors knew that pain
must be fought with pain.

It's quite simple: an array of needles pricking your arm
for a properly functioning heart and lungs.
Needles in the feet to ease insomnia and stress.
Needles between your eyes to fight infertility.
A little pain here,
and the effect is felt elsewhere
Once, a group of explorers set out to plant a flag on the South Pole,
a needle at the heel of the globe, in the middle of nowhere.
But before the mission was completed
a new world war had begun.
The impact of the needle was felt in the world's brain,
in the lobe responsible for short-term memory.
When Russia used ideology as acupuncture – a needle over the Urals –
it impacted the pancreas and the control of blood sugar:
America paid tenfold for whiskey during Prohibition,
and at post offices, copies of Joyce's
'immoral' *Ulysses* were stored for burning.

The universe functions as a single body. Stars form lines of needles
carefully pinned to a broad hairy back.
Their impact is felt in the digestive tract, each day
a new beginning. How can you begin a new day
not having fully absorbed yesterday's protein?
I was a child when my first teacher
mispronounced my last name twice. That pricked me like a needle.

A small needle in the earlobe. And suddenly,
my vision cleared –
I saw poetry,
the perfect disguise.

First Week of Retirement

This time of day, light spills from window ledges
like wine from chins at a bacchanal.
He was a general. But the man in the mirror is simply a soldier
waiting for his superior's signal
to zip the tent shut.

From the kitchen, the smell of something burning.
The daily newspaper, unopened, yellows on the couch.
And the cat, a stray cat in heat,
meows under the window.

God knows why the cat chooses to cry in his yard
filled with empty bottles and ribbons of cassette tape.
And only God knows why a sales agent
knocks on his door day after day
trying to sell him a Japanese knife set.

Damn cat! He shoved her once with his foot,
yet she still cries, this time on his roof.
And the sales agent won't leave:
'You get a free shaving kit with the knives!
You can't beat a deal like this!'

A nervous hand slides over his woundless body.
Nowhere to rest it. No sign as to when the weather might change.
'What the hell should I do with seventeen knives?!'

Does this sales agent who, like a cat,
can't distinguish red from green,
know that only a week ago
he led thousands of men
and that he had more stars pinned to his uniform
than teeth in his mouth?

A general during peacetime,
waiting for a war that never happened.

Everything under control, functional
like an electric shaver. A bonus.
But...where is life itself?
Where are the knives?

A Conversation with Charles Simic

Las Vegas. In a bar. A hybrid light half-red, half-orange
highlights vague parentheses on people's faces. Wrinkles.
I am sitting next to Charles Simic.
His last name is pronounced differently
in his new language than in his mother tongue;
the final consonants hardened along the way
like cardboard boxes drenched on the deck of a ship
only to dry again under another sun.

Someone is wiping beer foam from his beard.
You can't tell if it's already dark outside.
A nervous figure in the corner keeps trying his luck
on a machine, waiting for change to fall out.
And the music –
the music forms large air bubbles
under the skin.

We are both from the Balkans. Our countries are separated by
        mountains,
which seen from above, look peaceful like dozing elephants.
They take short naps. Because of their weight,
their bodies never find rest
and they turn from one side to the other
making it impossible for them
to all dream at the same time.

We chatted. Perhaps he spoke about literature, religion,
politics... perhaps.
It was terribly noisy. Impossible to follow a conversation.
So I only followed the timbre of his voice,
the deep, mature, inner timbre congested with calcium,
like drops of water falling from cave ceilings to the ground,

from earth to earth
the shortest journey for sound
but the longest
for us mortals.

The Business of Dying

People can tolerate everything –
theft, violence, injustice, murder...
But not suicide.

The one who killed himself broke the rules of the game,
ignoring the script
and everyone else's long waiting line.

His clothes weren't given away to the neighbours
and of course weren't burned. Burning them would release
the arrogant cloud of his Scottish fabric into the air.

'He was a coward,' someone said loudly.
'He was brave,' another said quietly. The rest
simply memorised a new flavour of death
on their tongues without swallowing
like a sommelier her wine.

Only a scrap of paper left behind,
written clearly, without secrets, no innuendos or pauses,
ending with 'I die' in the causative form of the verb. A grammatical
        terror;
he has just robbed them of mourning, the marinating salt
that could help them bear another six months of hibernation.

Some forgot to lock their gates that night
and dogs hardly barked.
Fear retreated, like periodontal disease
revealing the roots beneath gums.
They suddenly found themselves alone
and entirely insignificant.

Among other things, he had picked the wrong time: November,
when the body becomes paranoid of itself,
bleeding a dark coppery sweat from the same spot
(nobody owed him that either).
This is how suicide turns into a natural monument.

Metallic

1

We knew nothing back then about Santa,
but we knew Hasije, the ice cream vendor.

We'd press against the counter and before our eyes
a plump goddess out of Titian's vision appeared.
With a large wooden ladle, she scooped the ice cream
from the mixing machine into a stainless-steel pot.

We knew the number of beauty marks on her forearm
better than we knew the number of years we had lived.

When she put down the ladle, a storm of jangling coins
would blow to her face.
The tallest were the lucky ones;
the short ones were only coins that spun
as if hypnotised, and ended up forced into a corner.

No one ever saw Hasije
open or close the shop.
But the lorry drivers
confirmed that they stopped by for an espresso at dawn,
and late in the evenings, for cognac and a smoke.
'Impossible!' one of us protested.

To see Hasije, her icy-Saturnalian ring,
her sleeves rolled up to her armpits,
was a dream for us.
And just as a dream turns to smoke in the last instant,
some days when it was my turn, she shouted in a metallic voice:
'That's it. The ice cream's finished!'

And: 'I said, that's it! No more for today!'
But nobody would move.
And from the back of the line, the spinning coins
would turn aggressive and plea:
'One ice cream, *teta*!'
Because to those at the end of the line, to the powerless,
bad news is merely gossip,
and behind empty pots
a goddess becomes twice the goddess she was.

Many years later I returned
and asked about Hasije and the only ice cream shop in town.
They said the poor woman had a tumour
and couldn't survive it.

This is how it had to happen.
Local legends have only two options:
they must either flee, or die,
so we'll have a clean past to talk about.

2

The hospital's prostate hall smells of watermelon,
the cheapest fruit of the season.
He lifts his arm and presses a button.
'What's wrong?' enquires the half body of a nurse through the
        doorway.
Nothing. It's the visiting hour.
His feet are icy cold.

In classical drama, his name would be King Lear.
But in real life he's simply someone
who rarely looks at the door.

Today's a holiday, when women
used to wash the doorsteps with lime
and children returned home late, cheeks bursting red
from watching turkey fights.
Grounded as punishment,
they'd wipe their running noses on their sleeves,
and when they pressed their eyes to their knees,
they'd see a vision of an amber desert
without people.

And, by the way, he once had two little girls,
(or three?) to whom he'd tell the bedtime story
of the migrating swans, the only one he knew.

But, as usual, at the wrong moment,
the hospital food cart brings the other
half of the nurse into the room.
'Are you ready? I brought soup and peas!'
She enters without knocking. No one knocks here.

First of all, you need a door to knock on.
And to have a door, you need a woman's finger
with a fake diamond ring on it
and a metallic voice: 'Quick, get up, you're late for work!'

teta: an Albanian term used by children to refer to adult women.

The Body's Delay

Really, they say, it was her bottles of perfume,
her hesitation to leave Versailles without her favourite fragrances
(when horses neighed danger in the courtyard),
that cost Marie Antoinette her life –
a brief delay that changed history.

One trip my luggage
arrived in Dublin two days after me.
My underwear, size seven shoes, toiletries,
hair dryer, nightgown, valium,
novel with dog-eared pages,
and the medium-petite dresses,
revolving alone on empty conveyor belts
at the wrong airports.

The body is slow, clumsy; it rarely surprises you.
It takes you to places
your imagination has explored
long in advance.

And you may falsely believe
that when you're young, healthy, and beautiful.
the body leads the way.
Remember how often it's been abandoned,
like a supporting actor on the red carpet
dismissed by cameras.

Clumsy, yet sly,
the body hunts for the moment when it can catch up with you.
So it was in my moments of hesitation
when my children were born. And my garden expanded
with other seasons, signposts, fences,
along with other dilemmas.

And just when you believe that it is clumsier than ever,
heavier from age, sclerotic, stuck in arterial traffic,
precisely at that point
does the body lead the way.

Because the body has no nostalgia.
And you're the one left behind like a pillar of salt
when there's nothing left to worship.

Two by Two

He grew up in a small town by the water,
where people answer a question
with another question.

Long summers, rebellious without cause,
and along the river's edge, leaves greying like sideburns.

On Sundays, four women wash clothes
in the river, slapping their men's shirts on the rocks.
Four reflections imitate the actions,
taking revenge on husbands who don't exist.

Lost, at the edge of the water, a confused child
listens to his mother calling and doesn't respond –
isolation an artefact that can't be reproduced.

His father cuts his hair in the yard without a mirror
on one of those days when he's in a good mood
and the sophism of grapes distils on the tongue.
His scissors make no mistakes;
they clean up carefully around the ears, above the eyes
(this was the whole point anyway).
Sitting on the chair, his feet hanging without touching the ground,
the boy feels safe. The future cannot find him here
the way a dog can't pick up someone's scent in water.

Clepsydra, the one who measures time,
has no favourites among her clients.

At night, the voice of the river is totalitarian
like his father's alcoholic breath
that blows against his neck after a haircut.

And he doesn't dare look back at what he did.
His vision doubles: two pasts,
two versions of the truth,
two women to fall in love with,
two lives to escape.
But which of them is real? Which an illusion?

Gloves

I am leaving this Park Central Hotel room on Seventh Avenue.
I switch the lights off and my eyes search for the window. Like a
    surgical mask,
it's hard to pluck a smile from the reflection, or a hint of compassion,
    a farewell.

In a few minutes, a deluge of cleaning staff will take over:
mops, detergents, clean sheets, the acidic accent of the language
    they speak,
the electric vacuum whose metropolitan appetite
sucks three days out of my life in mere seconds.

They wear yellow plastic gloves. The same colour gloves
a woman who cleans my colleague's office uses,
along with the seven types of detergents: for bacteria, skin cells,
    notes,
telephone calls, aspirations, and mainly, for his name.
No one called him by name.
A name, though, has a very mild freezing point;
it can only be smothered for a short time.

And as you leave the plane, the yellow gloves enter from another
    door.
Sterilisation grows even more powerful here:
seats disinfected after long intercontinental nights
(a fact never included in biographies)
and headphones after movies watched over the ocean.

The nurse changing an intravenous line in the hospital
appears a little more human.
Her gloves are opaque. With her eyes on the patient's
    electrocardiogram,

she waits quietly for the hills on the screen to iron out.
Behind tears, the patient's nephew
hides a wicked joy –
the leather armchair that faces the garden.

Hygiene, hygiene, hygiene.
How quickly the world hurries to clean up every trace!

Remnants are events only to an archaeologist:
he doesn't require gloves to handle a five-thousand-year-old
        skeletal jaw.
There's no risk of infection. And no hesitation
in my mother's ponderous narrative
and dry-cleaned voice: 'What's done is done.'

Some call it 'universal detergent', while others simply 'time'.
And yet, pay attention to the instructions: 'Keep out of reach of
        children!'

I Came, I Saw, I Left...

Hunched inside a forty-five degree corner,
eyes glued to the cartoons
on the TV screen, the light
projecting onto his face.
He could be a statue in the park
though not exactly. This is my father
who has chosen the expression I'll remember him by
for the rest of my life.
No one expects anything from him.
He might continue to sit like that
for another million years,
a fossil inside amber,
surrounded by forgetfulness and forgiveness.

And the profiles of my grandparents?
They posed for twenty minutes
standing in front of a daguerreotype camera
until the smiles evaporated from their faces
leaving them exposed
and bitterly dignified.

John Coltrane, on the other hand, never stares at you.
It's difficult to remember one of his gestures or looks.
He simply plays the saxophone.
Measures time with his feet. Vigilant.
His melancholy intervenes at the right moment,
like wrapping a nude woman in a jacket.

Van Gogh sketched portraits of people's backs,
naming them 'Orphan Man with Long Overcoat',
'Orphan with Top Hat'...
Or did those backs sketch him?

It's a question of speed
and depends on who was faster.

When my three-year-old daughter Lea
needed a passport photo,
I took her in my arms and we posed together,
as she was afraid of the camera.
The photographer cut out her face from mine,
snipping away the context.
She feels calm inside that false identity,
and has yet to discover the betrayal.

Joyful youth, their feet teetering from too much beer,
spill out of a club and disappear
into the wide *métis* cheekbones of midnight.
Anxious sleep-wasters,
they stumble through night's buckram robe
like statues at an inauguration.

Meanwhile, statues of heroes and rulers in city squares
have won the game against time.
With the triumphant expression of Julius Caesar,
all of them say: 'I came, I saw, I conquered.'
But wasn't he the same Caesar
who, with bulging eyes and a knife at his throat,
spoke his last: 'You too, Brutus?'

Index

Days were never this long before.
Their whiteness a lactose too difficult to break down.
He dozes wherever he can. Gets upset only when lunch isn't ready
    on time.
Speaks a little less each day and moves from one sentence to
    another
without argument, as if drifting between rooms
in a house without corridors.
Yet sometimes he asks questions like:
'What did God have in mind when he made man?'
A rhetorical question you don't need to answer.

He falls asleep as fast as a book that drops from his hand.
It is said that the most ordinary among us is a written book
that exists in heaven, a book so huge
that human eyes cannot read it.
That's where everything
is recorded – what we've done, said, thought, felt,
even what hasn't happened yet. Who could imagine
that a human body – some square centimetres
that were once only a cell –
could contain so much space for history?

He understands other people less, including his wife,
the book he's lived with cover to cover
written in two different languages
and placed on the shelf
according to the index.

We need a third language to communicate.
A language with idioms and innuendos we don't recognise.

A camouflage
of colours to blend in with our surroundings
of tones to conceal weakness
of temperature to shield ourselves against those who hurt us
(some prey are exposed by their own warmth).

Now he is a closed book.
No time to add or revise anything.
All that remains is touch,
the touch between the leather covers,
the feeling he gets on elbows, knees, hair,
the laughter when his arms cross over her neck
at an outdoor cinema
as they watch the movie under the summer sky.

Transit Terminal

No sky except the floor beneath your feet
scraped by the dyslexia of passengers
travelling for the first time.

Wheelchairs
aggressively cut through the terminal –
their cold comet tails
cloud up the display windows of duty-free shops.

And yet 'Marc Jacobs', 'Louis Vuitton', 'Armani',
'Chanel' are always someone else's fantasy
(Think carefully before you step in!)
served under a Scandinavian neon sun
on a deceptive cloud of parquet.

Inside luxurious smoking rooms
Camel ads offer an adventure in the desert.
Characters chain-smoke
without exchanging glances –
the first act in a theatre of the absurd.

Music. Oh, you can never tell where it's coming from –
maybe from the fire sprinklers above
or from our own soul pockets.

The last call for late passengers disrupts the tune.
Nothing threatening in the announcer's voice.
If you miss this flight, you can take the next one
sooner or later.
Leaving here is unavoidable.

And it's karma that constantly forces me towards corners,
sitting on the floor and watching everything from afar,
as one of Archimedes' disciples
who know the secret to balance:
what you lose in weight, you gain in distance.

Live Music

Nothing consoles you more before sleep
than this pub of cheap beer and *live* music,
the callous voice of the singer, the lyrics
thrown forcefully together inside *rima pobre*.

The beer, too. An argument in the corner,
marks the only difference between the days of the week
and Friday night. And the phosphorescence of free, platonic sex.
What happens on board, stays on board.

At the edge of the table, wet receipts
with a circled digit at the end
are indulgence's shortcut from purgatory to paradise
(not worth doubting any of this).

A sweet nothing of apathy and a mockery
latches onto the singer.
'Oh man, she started too high, won't be able to reach the refrain!'
'You think so?'
'You wanna bet?'
When nobody really needs to hear the refrain.
They're here precisely for the emptiness
the vast emptiness in a divey pub
like the white, fluffy inside of artisan bread
and its smooth crust on the outside.

Exiting this place is less than ceremonial.
Imagine sitting in a barber shop
and the barber – sympathetically, according to ritual –
gives you a slap on the neck after finishing your cut:
'Get up now, it's someone else's turn!'

Ramesses' Last Journey

Because of threatening floods
they broke the statue of Ramesses into blocks
and moved it to a safe and sequestered place
far from where it was created.

For many hours
his Egyptian nose
hung between sky and earth
drawing the attention of a derrick-man and a part-time porter.
His sceptre hung there, too, the sceptre of a man who once said,
'I carried away those whom my sword had spared
as numerous captives pinioned like birds before my horses.'

In a few days
all his broken parts will reunite
and he will be the Great Ramesses again,
the star of morning and evening,
ambushed by the camera's sanguine flashes
like knives in a sailors' tavern.

But the intelligent eye
will not see the sculpture itself but the geometric
cuts between the blocks, the transportation scars,
asking, 'How heavy was it?' and 'How did they get it here?'

Like the folded lines of an overused map
where mountains were flattened a long time past
and roads and their conventional symbols have disappeared,
the names of cities coagulated.

Statue or statuette,
the last confession doesn't belong to the pharaoh
but to those who shouldered the burden,
to the blind map circulating in pieces
that shows our only landscape
and the speed with which we traversed it.

FROM

Homo Antarcticus

(2015)

Homo Antarcticus

> The wild will keep calling and calling forever in your ears.
> You cannot escape the 'little voices'.
>
> FRANK WILD

1

Here I rest, in South Georgia.
A few feet of evolution away
lie the graves of whale hunters, pointing north.
A white fence shields them from elephant seals
and their apocalyptic screams that each day warn
of the end of the world, or maybe the beginning...

I survived five expeditions to the Pole.
The one before last, 'Imperial Trans-Antarctica', nearly killed me.
For two years I put up with the ice – no man can reap or sow
        these fields.
And, unlike farmers, I didn't even need to ask God for rain,
because ice is sated
and more desolate than the Sahara.

I survived distance. Wrote one message after another
beginning with a capital letter and a 'P.S.' at the end.
My own personal post office under my pillow
closed for two years already, on holiday.

I survived six-month-long polar days and nights;
to this day, I don't know which one was worse.

My epitaph is simple. Carved in granite:
FRANK WILD
18 April 1873
19 August 1939
'Shackleton's
Right Hand Man'

For those cast away here
by a defect in the engine of the ship
or nostalgia of the womb.

2

Ah, yes…in the beginning was the ship. The ship stuck in ice.
    Endurance.
Ships are women. They prefer soft seas.
In the best-case scenario, she's called *La Santa María*
and she throws you, like Columbus, on some foreign shore.

But if you get too close to her…

The very day after
we washed her deck with warm water and soap,
warmed her arteries with gin,
stroked her lower back with our surrogate songs,
shaved our beards and exposed the illiterate lines on our faces,
she took off.

And from the shore,
we saw how she broke her ribs, sinking,
aft first, so fast we didn't even have time to pray,
leaving behind her ash-tree fragrance
and faux pearls on the water.

'Such a woman!' someone laughed bitterly,
'She knows when to leave so as not to be forgotten.'

3

A woman, naturally, has no business there.
Antarctica is a masculine continent –
male penguins keep the eggs warm,

73

the moon stands up on the street to urinate
after being kicked out of the tavern,
the cold like a cut-throat razor, dulled for three thousand years,
and the sled dogs, the huskies,
we kill with a single bullet
so they won't starve to death. In this way,
we instil a little character into the new land
before the arrival of conquistadors, thieves,
assassins, missionaries, prostitutes,
the first invading army of every continent.

Antarctica is a man's continent,
because only a man chooses to break into the darkness of the mind
by conquering the body,
as Amundsen and Scott did, their glory
reaching to the apex of ecstasy.
Zero degree of geographical latitude,
utter collapse.

4

Hunger is overestimated. The stomach functions much like the
    brain:
when it has nothing to think about, it feeds off memories.
It can last three days just thinking of a single biscuit.
But those who have a better memory, meaning a much stronger
    acidity,
can go on for months
remembering a slice of prosciutto, two fried eggs,
sweetly folding their eyelids like napkins after a meal.

Then hallucinations begin. Banquets. Easter supper.
Feet move impatiently under the table;
the scent of rosemary wafts from a platter
and two clean serving hands with burns here and there.

That's when you feel grief-stricken
and you attack the seals and penguins with your
alpine knives and shoes like a madman
in an empty amphitheatre.
Or is this, too, a hallucination,
and in this case not ours
but Antarctica's?

And when clarity finally returns,
both stomach and brain
notice only their own deep wrinkles.

   5

Blubber, blubber, seal's blubber.
Blubber that keeps your spirits alive, rendering it for fuel, for light,
blubber to mask the body's foul odour,
– a mixture of doubt, hope, and ammonia.
And if you have nothing better to do,
think of a cow's thigh hanging at the butcher's,
its delicate streak of fat
like a silk ribbon.

I survived even this sarcasm.

And every night, before bed,
we read recipes to each other
one of a few things we secretly rescued
from the ship before she sank,
as if these items were her lingerie.

What a show it was!
What pathos in pronouncing *prosciutto, sugar, omelette!*
What sensuality in *milk, parsley, cinnamon!*
We made these words up ourselves.
Nothing exists until its moment of absence.

But first, in order to warm up our mouths
like actors before going on stage,
we'd repeat mechanically, palates dry,
'Bless us, O Lord,
and this food we've received through your mercy.'

6

It was the Romans who spoiled the word
studying rhetoric
before anatomy and mathematics:
Vir bonus dicendi peritus
'The good man skilled in speaking' (Marcus Porcius Cato)

But in Antarctica, words are measured differently: by calories!
With a simple greeting you lose five calories,
just as many to keep a fire burning for a full minute.
And a Ciceronian argument can consume a whole day's nutrition;
think carefully before you open your mouth.

The word is overestimated.

Sometimes it's enough to avert your eyes from your shoes
to imply 'gangrene';
and a vague exchange of glances between men
is enough to understand that the ice is cracking beneath your feet
and death is closer than your fingers.

7

Stretched smooth from end to end – such is Antarctica. In fact,
even a baby's skin looks withered by comparison.
No emotions. No regrets. No warnings.
Either fight or die.

My father was like this more or less. A teacher at a village school.
In classrooms that smelled of sheep-wool pullovers
drying on the body. And eyes that moved freely
in their hollows, like toes
inside an older sibling's shoes.

Unlike the Romans,
my father preached about justice and honour,
his hands folded behind his back.
His shoulders seemed twice as wide
as his worn jacket.

I inherited his sharp, grey gaze,
and his soft voice.
Eyes that say 'Go' and a voice that says 'Stay'.
You never know which one to trust.

8

And mother? Oh, she was simply Captain Cook's niece,
– the great James Cook –
from morning to night
when she washed, swept, dug potatoes from the garden,
fixed her husband's tie on Sundays
even from her bed, while in labour.
She never spoke of this. As it wasn't necessary.
People speak of what they have, not what they are.

She was a tailor. Measured everyone's perimeter with a glance;
erred only on the width of one's neck, an unknown strength.
Her large scissors followed
the white chalk line on the cloth so precisely. 'Snip!'
She said little. Her silence followed the white outlines
of another tailor,
over a fabric much older than she was.

But now that I think of it,
how did the poor woman respond to her friends asking,
'Where is your son?'
'He's exploring the world.'
'And what does he bring back from there?'
'Himself, alive, I hope.'
'What's the point of returning empty-handed after two years?'

Was she at least a little proud of me? Of her Frank?
Certainly not. She was Captain Cook's niece.
The past always conquers.

9

I was the first of thirteen children.
And as a rule, each of them
eyed one of my belongings.
One eyed my bed near the window
that overlooked the water where frogs lived
and asparagus grew on the shore.
Another eyed my green jacket bought with borrowed money,
poker cards, a fishing net,
my wicker chair with the damaged back.
Another whistled my favourite tune
'What Will We Do with a Drunken Sailor?'
without reaching the refrain.
And yet another envied the basement
– that place I occupied in my father's heart –
with its elm door hanging by a single hinge.

But the time hasn't come to leave home just yet,
until your own brother begins to use your shaving kit
and dreams of the same girl.

10

What shaving kit? Antarctica makes you grow a double-beard,
as if you were a hundred-year-old grave.
And, while you remember wasting time queuing at the barber's,
another beard grows, a red one.

Here, each body part works for itself:
the stomach, hands, intestines, eyes...
The unity of the body is overestimated, too.

Only skin pulls everything together like a sled.
The skin? Which skin? Man loses his first skin
to his first love, like the snake early in spring
on a thorn-apple bush that blocks the way.
From that point on he stops counting the rest.

11

I don't know why it was named 'Elephant Island',
when it answered the ocean with the cries of a she-wolf.
We could only make out her sly teats under her belly. After some
    time,
if she didn't kill us first, we'd begin to cry like wolves ourselves.

Twenty-two people. Packed next to one another under two
    inverted boats
like notes in Bach's 'Come, Sweet Death, Come Blessed Rest',
with more pauses, a dramatic suffocation between breaths.
A dry, hacking cough was a sign of life. Or the delirious mutterings
    of someone
dreaming aloud of 'ice' in the middle of ice,
after they had cut off his toes.

But the hardest moment arrives in the morning,
when, with shut eyes and plugged nostrils,

as if drinking your own urine
you recycle the same lie for four months straight:
'Men, pack up your stuff! The boss might arrive today!'

And they obeyed me. Packed carefully each day from the start,
leaving nothing sharp in the folds of their bags,
nothing that would spoil the line between fact and fiction.

It was a time when
routine grew more powerful than hope.

12

Fish in the ocean toyed with our citizenship.
On the seventh mile, we left our medals behind, class ranks,
along with the dogs, potatoes, and a camera.
We made fire out of money
and kept only a single metal coin each
so that archaeologists might trace us more easily centuries later.
On Elephant Island, we had to bid farewell even to tobacco,
tobacco which reminded us of village alleyways
and walks home after midnight.

Time glided above us without touching a single strand of our hair –
nonexistent, as if gliding above ancient cities,
exposing the solemnity of our white bones
and crickets on absent walls.

That's when the ten commandments deserted us:
'Do not steal', 'Do not lie', 'Do not covet',
'Honour your parents'…
save one of them perhaps,
the one about the holiness of Sunday.

We already had nothing. We belonged to no one.
An entirely new species: HOMO ANTARCTICUS.
A scientific proof that 'forgotten' and 'free'
mean the same thing.

13

Two years after returning from the world of the dead,
you find your house taken over by another tenant
and the rent tripled,
the commemorative plaque nailed to the gate:
'Here lived F.W.'
And your lover, or better, ex-lover,
for the same reason,
in the arms of another
three times more handsome.

You see your own image sold at an auction.
Artefact. Original. '*Brrramp!* Sold!' The price so high
you can't afford it. But even if you could,
you're an illegal customer,
holding a death certificate in your hand.

And you find your parents turned into winter trees
their eyes fixed on a large cloud of plaster.
They don't expect visitors. Best not disturb them.
Let their leaves fall quietly where they will
let the crow's nest remain in the armpit of a branch,
where it has always been.

Perhaps you should take a shortcut, start over.
Or you know what? There's a war going on nearby, they say.
Go there instead!
But this time die better.

14

War's never satisfied with flesh.
Fresh, branded, smoked,
with or without blood,
blue blood, dark, thick, whatever kind.
And frozen blood like yours
could store at minus 40 degrees Celsius,
viruses from 1914 unscathed,
and the map of the old Empire
and Scott's hurt ego
and old coins minted with the head of Edward VII,
and Browning's poetry and the epic of the unknown,
like an envelope inside an envelope,
all making you the ideal candidate.

Back on the ship, ammunition everywhere,
sailing through the cold Northern seas
where you had to learn a new language.
A new language is like a fish:
first, you need to remove its spine
in order to chew it.

Unlike in Antarctica,
one's purpose in war is clear: kill or be killed,
though sometimes it's the same difference.

Baltic nights gave you what Antarctica refused you:
the other half of the celestial sphere.
You met Vera, the widow of a tea plantation owner,
a character out of a baroque novel, her pupils blurred with dusk,
and the ritual of mourning fitted perfectly to her body
like a final journey.

15

A man charmed by a glacier,
who knows too well the flawless forms of her body,
feels her eavesdropping gaze even when asleep,
her clean and distant breath
and her heart, a piece of ice, that melts inside a cigarette case
heated for drinking water,
finds it difficult to marry a real woman,
to marry Vera.
And Africa.

I bought land. Barren. Hundreds of acres. In Zululand.
I didn't fare well with tobacco. Planted cotton instead,
chose bodily peace rather than meditation.
My nearest neighbour lived 45 miles away. White, *of course.*
And my fate, never blended with the blacks,
those beautiful statues, wrapped in straw.
I heard them nod off during lunch break,
like the oars of a boat,
in complete sync.
They knew where they were heading.
But I didn't.

And I was right. It didn't take long
before drought, floods, worms
destroyed everything. The bank left me only my own beard
and the malarial shadow of a baobab. Apart from other things,
Vera filled out divorce papers. The woman in the yellow dress,
yellow as quinine, yellow as the sigh of a hinge at dusk,
the woman married to the hero
who now can't even manage a small plot of land.

16

The man in front of me
– my master I call 'Boss' –
is newly shaved, and dressed in a striped tie and jacket
as if the Prince of Wales or Fred Astaire,
a style that arrives here two years late.
He asks me to serve whiskey to clients at the bar
and chat them up
using their jargon, gestures,
sentences uninterrupted by mosquitoes,
and the abstract rhetoric of the Depression years.
And, to be frank,
he pays me for the latter.

But what do I know,
what does a survivor know about the art of living,
for which new instincts are needed, new muscles
and other kinds of heart valves?

Furthermore,
how can I obey such a spick-and-span *boss*,
having known the smoky *gods* of Antarctica
who recognise each other solely by the nose
and can end rebellions with a glance
and count the deaths as members of the crew?
How can I take orders from a boss whose name isn't *Shackleton*?

17

'Second in command', 'Lieutenant', 'Shackleton's right-hand'...

What did she see so clearly in me,
my drama teacher in elementary school,
when she'd always assign me the role of Father Joseph,
of Gaspar the Magi offering Jesus frankincense,

or of John the Baptist always there to clear the path?
What did she see in my metallic pupils, baritone voice, infrequent
    speech
as if scissors, bandage, and iodine
inside a first aid kit?

Under Antarctica's naked sky, each of us followed his own star.
Even the carpenter, his own heraldic calling.
You didn't need much to feed them;
just a few crusts of insomnia and the tents' punctured holes.

My star was weak; you could hardly see it
hidden behind another larger, troubled star
like a calm valley that appears behind jagged peaks
more attractive when absent.

18

What happened afterwards can be told in a few words:
I worked in a mine; earth's warm heart,
happened to be crueller than her frozen brain.
I laid railway tracks South, always towards the Unknown.
It was like playing only two strings on a violin: joy and sorrow,
fatefully blending at the horizon.

I repaired houses. Another waste of time.
I never understood their weak points,
just as you can't make out eyes from genitals or mouth
in some underwater creatures.

And when I was left penniless,
I gave lectures about Antarctica,
water gurgling in my gullet every five words, for those few
who listened patiently to an adventure of survival.

Then Bea arrived. Or sweet Beatrice.
It was easy to grant her what I had left in my heart
– that set of heavy museum keys –
with no fear she might lose them.

Tired lungs and liver
could barely follow my split image
of bust and bottle of booze.
Like a prophet in the last circle of Dante's *Inferno*
I carried my own decapitated head in hand.

My ashes were lost at the base of a church. No one thought of them.
It was a time of war. Another world war. The second
one not knowing what to do with her own ashes either.

19

Some of us died in the war. Others took to the sea again,
the grey, cracked waters of the South,
decks perspiring fuel and alcohol.
Our random itineraries. Full-time melancholics.

For months in Antarctica,
we waited for our shadow to return
and consumed that question you ask yourself only once in your
     lifetime,
the way one consumes chickenpox.

And the rest of the time,
we counted the scars left on our faces,
with a gesture you could call indifferent and epic,
or childlike.

Something Bigger than Us

The Eskimos have numerous different words for 'snow':
the freshly fallen, the stepped on, the aged,
the piled up in heaps, the rotten one
left over from the previous winter.
As if near-sighted,
they're able to distinguish different shades of white:
the nothingness, the emptiness, the present of an eternity,
and the eternity of the present.

Where I come from,
we have four different words for 'evening'.
Funny, but the one that fits best
is borrowed from a foreign language
brought over by invaders, not by spice merchants,
and it rhymes with 'lilacs'.

Where I come from,
there's only one word for 'grief' and for 'water'
and both take the form of the containers that hold them:
each to their own fate, each to their own grief.

The Greeks have four different words for 'love',
like the four stakes of a tent
that assure you a spot in this world
if not today, maybe tomorrow.

According to anthropologists,
until a century ago, my people
had no word for 'love',
only a clever, naive doubt:
'It's something bigger than us, right?'

A doubt performed with the rhetorical gesture of a King
who asks questions and expects
answers to arrive only in his dreams.

Menelaus's Return

After Troy,
no one bothered to mention my return to Sparta –
not Homer, not even the historians.
Somewhere, someone mumbled something about it lasting eight years.
They had no time for me; they were busy with Odysseus',
Idomeneo's, and Agamemnon's retaliation.
One of them had to kill the conqueror of the throne,
the other his son in order to reward Poseidon,
and the third, with a knife to his back,
would write his wife's story.
My return ends here,
on this ship with my soldiers
who clench their armour still stinking of smoke,
and with my slaves who don't care where we go,
or if we'll ever reach our destination,
and with a lot of pride, my honour regained,
and with Helen there on the deck, constantly seasick.
She's mine now, but I have no idea what to do with her.

Someone said I came close to Crete, but the winds pushed me off to
    Egypt
where I waited and waited for the right wind to return.
But it never came.
Someone else said that I returned to Sparta, because Telemachus
had no one else to ask about his father
(undoubtedly, this would make sense on paper).
But the truth is
that I continued to wander on open seas, forgotten,
on history's waters,
even though, there, in the palace, they waited for me,
my servants uselessly heating up my house, starting over each day,
uselessly slaughtering livestock they consumed themselves.

Patris now doesn't exist.
Not because of a curse from the gods,
but because with revenge
everything ends. The curtain falls.
And peace is never a motif.

Here's my wish for you, dear reader:
May your revenge arrive as late as possible!
Believe me, afterwards you'll be forgotten,
forgotten amongst the living and the dead.

The Railway Boys

Of course they're blond, all of them blond,
easy to distinguish one another
among the grease, smoke, and coal dust.
They ride the train's whistle effortlessly,
as if hunting buffalo.
They know each whistle's tricks.
From a distance they can tell which train
heads to the cold north
and which to the south; they know
which railcar carries mail, and which
carries passengers who will never return.

When the freight train arrives,
they hurry to climb
and enjoy a piece of the sky
lying on their backs atop wood logs.
This is only half the journey –
now they're closer to the first star
in the sky than to their homes.

This is the first test of manhood.
Everything else comes later, behind a broken boxcar,
with the girl with rust-coloured hair.
Who is she? The first lover with a beautiful buck tooth
has no name of her own – only the one she was christened with.
Same with the second lover... And the third...
No clothes are needed for the one prepared
to wear his own father's clothes,
not needed for the son of Aaron,
whose only blasphemy
would ban him from the land of milk and honey.

Of course they're blond, all blond,
the railway boys. For them,
everything is possible. See how the first railcar returns
last, and the last one first,
when the locomotive switches tracks?

'What's it like up north?'
'The people wear hides and have blue veins.'
'And south? What have you heard?'
'There, people think with their hearts and speak in gestures.'
Over the hot rails, the air, like a concave mirror,
magnifies their slim bodies and the words 'hide' and 'heart'
grow blurry and quiet.

And against his will, each one of them
will marry the wrong girl,
each girl with eyes full of a long winter.
Among naked trees
it's impossible to lose the way home.

As time passes,
the train whistles die out,
the buffalo-clouds of smoke turn into white, fluffy puppies.
And the sleeves of the fathers' never-worn cloaks
point out a north and a south
equally impossible.

Metamorphosis

Summer draws near.
With it, a yearning for life
even though you're still alive. Here's another chance
to get closer to...
get closer to whom? To what?
You can't even name it.

When you were a child, you used to draw a square
with a chimney puffing blue smoke, and you'd call it home.
A yellow ball – the sun, a red circle with a tail you'd call an apple,
and a squashed apple, the heart.

Once upon a time, everything was simple.
Objects are still the same – we've only added
the names of things the way we give intimate nicknames
to streets and corners in a city we've lived in for years,
unable to make it our own.

And later, in the absence of hope,
we turn objects back into abstract forms,
into what they once were
in their original state:
a house puffing blue smoke, a blinding yellow ball,
an apple and a heart.

When there's no hope left,
we turn objects into art –
a sermon we leave behind
for the generations to come.

January 1, Dawn

After the celebrations,
people, TV channels, telephones,
the year's recently corrected digit
finally fall asleep.

Between the final night and the first dawn
a jagged piece of sky
as if viewed from the open mouth of a whale.
Inside her belly and inside the belly of time,
there's no point worrying.
You glide gently along. She knows her course.
Inside her, you are digested slowly, painlessly.

And if you're lucky, like Jonah,
at some point she'll spit you out on dry land
along with heaps of inorganic waste.

Everything sleeps. A sweet hypothermic sleep.
But those few still awake
might hear the melancholy creaking of a wheelbarrow,
someone stealing stones from a ruin
to build new walls just a few feet away.

Ageing

It approaches. I can feel it without seeing it,
like feeling the presence of waves nearby.
All the world's rivers spill into the sea
even your own, even the sweet waters
that in a few seconds turn salty
and bitter as hell in the deep.

Every day the mirror wakes up in a bad mood.
An endless field of frost glistens
on the cabbages beyond the window.

It's the late harvest and nothing more.
You're alarmed:
Do you have enough food to survive the winter?
Enough to chew on, enough memories?
Although you'll need a strong stomach
for some of them.

Ask your mother what she knows about ageing.
Ask the elderly women of your family
lined up so beautifully
like silver cutlery in a cardboard box
waiting for a dinner that may never happen...

Ask them, how did they manage it?
Perhaps they will give you advice.
Or extend a hand to you,
that same warm, clammy, deceiving reach
that once pierced your ear as a child:
'It doesn't hurt a bit. Just a little sting.'

They have nothing to give.
Ageing is too personal
like the handkerchief, the razor, a pair of dentures.
They don't know that the elderly once had their own god, Saturn,
who looked after them during their free time
after the harvest, a meditation on time and feasts.

It approaches... It will go on for a long while, leisurely,
like a symphony that fills a radio channel in the late night hours,
rarely interrupted by brief news,
unapologetic, then continuing on again
where it left off, at Toccata and Fugue,
played by a solo flute.

Fishermen's Village

Squinty, salt-dusted windows face the distance.
They all look seaward.

Every third person here has the same name:
perhaps the name of a godparent
who cut her first lock of hair
before the wind thickened it,
or a stranger's name...
The locals, by the way, welcome the strangers,
because they were told
that one of them who once walked barefoot on water
used to load the sardine boats
with swift hands.

Foreigners are easily identified;
unlike the locals, their clothes are white, blue, jet black.
And sometimes,
they make you a gift of rosaries or cigars.
Once, one of them
left a pair of shoes behind
and the whole village gathered to play the lottery.
When someone with an already good pair of shoes won,
the young men who had been keenly following the show,
kicked the sand in anger,
'What the hell? It's not fair!'

Sand everywhere. All day long,
overturned boats on the shore
eat sand. Night stars feed on the sand.
The boats beached here since the last war
people remember brought
Omega watches strapped

to soldiers' wrists, and herpes
that spread from flesh to flesh
faster than wind
and faster than famine.

Cats purr behind doors.
Streets reek of fish and yet there are no fish.
Noontime, a man dozes on a sofa in the yard.
His wife sits at his feet, mending
the net with needle and thread,
which she cuts with her teeth.

Eyes half-open, he gazes at her
realising here is the real cause: the large hole in the net,
a hole first torn two thousand years ago after a prosperous fishing
    night,
when things were sorted out much like they are today:
some cursed with luck and some blessed with mercy.

Commit to Memory

These words are carved on the gravestone
of a Roman woman from 135 BC:
'Her parents named her Claudia.
She loved her husband dearly.
She bore two sons.
Was charming in conversation, and patient.
Kept a good house. Spun wool.'

The women I've known
can be described just as plainly with a single line:
M. who shined her copper pots and pans with sand.
L. who dreamed so much about her sons she was punished with a
    short life.
S. who made the best pickles.
H. who wouldn't shut up about her brother's mysterious death.
K. who used to peel fuzz off of faces with an egg-and-sugar mask.
F. the first to discover that a white dress goes best with yellow roses.
D. who ironed a perfect line on her husband's sleeves,
even when she knew he was going out with another woman.
P. who got along well with her mother-in-law.
S. who had an abortion every six months.
T. with a sweet laugh and always a run on her stockings.
N. who roasted good coffee when she had any.
R. who secretly used to sell her own blood.
Z. who picked up her son's guts with her own hands
the day he was hit by a freight train.

With a brief single line
like an old telegram, twenty cents a word,
and full of typing errors made by the post office staff.
As if that were the only way to remember them.

With a single, uninterrupted line
like Don Quixote in Picasso's hands.

You think it's that easy?

Cities

Cities are more or less the same:
lights, garbage, broken windows on the first floor of the music school,
street vendors, banks with red marble staircases,
bus stops, the smell of freshly baked bread equalising all,
bridges, women who age in their eyes and men who wither in their
    voices,
billboards, grudges that rot in vegetable cases on street markets,
rain staining roof tiles and bleaching graves,
a municipal band that's been playing 'The March of the Tartars' for
    thirty years,
the clocktower with its head in the clouds like a dervish in a trance,
    fresh lemonade,
and an ambulance parked between two worlds.

From the centre, gradually, my house and everyone else's
shifts to the periphery,
towards the city's limbs, its hands
not needing a language
to point out where it hurts or itches.

Each city taught you something:
the first about death at a train station – in broad daylight;
the second, how to live;
and the third,
the agnostic respite between the two.

You conquered the first one at night, in the dark;
the tame snakes on pharmacy walls
showed you the way.
The other, much earlier, without buttoning yourself.
A new accent split your face in two
like the line that parts your hair.

Each city left you with a scar:
The first a scratch on your eyebrow;
the second your hardened shoulders;
and the third, some logical gaps in your syntax.

But you left no mark on them.
Cities don't recognise you until the moment you flee,
when you escape in a hurry
and leave behind a single shoe,
abandoning the magic trick halfway through.

Anatomical Cut

Rexhep's knife is razor sharp. He's a third generation butcher.
Effortlessly, with its fine tip, he separates flesh from bone,
thigh from shoulder, heart from ribs,
a kosher day from another 'it could have been worse'
through an anatomical cut.

An unsold calf head hanging on a hook
acts as a pledge between the living and the dead
until evening.

Some clients show no respect, demanding, 'Take out the fat!'
the same way you would ask someone
to wipe their shoes carefully before entering the house.
Others simply love to chat.

From his father he learned how to cut without losses
and other small secrets of the trade,
secrets stolen but not mentioned
like how to slam meat on the scale, fast and hard.
A small deceit; just an ounce. No big deal.

His life is simple, made up of speed and knives,
knives sharpened with care each morning
so that, later in heaven, it will be easier
to piece the past back together on Judgement Day.

But when he returns home
with his hands and the status quo washed of blood,
he calculates the finances for studies
his son has no wish to complete;
he plans to buy a house where the stench of meat
won't conjure crows in his dreams,

and before sleeping, forcefully pulls his wife's hips towards him,
just her hips, and the hand on the scale points to an ounce of
    excess.

Small secrets of self-deceit no one ever talks about –
not even a father who knows the world better than anyone else,
from inside-out, entrails and all.

Self-portrait in Woven Fabrics

My life is a wardrobe
where the clothes are picked out
with a quick glance and hardly
ever with the slightest touch.

This never-worn silk shirt
wants a man's jacket over its shoulders
to end its flowering moment.
It hasn't bloomed yet and never will.
Throw it away, don't think twice!

This décolleté acrylic blouse
matches a smile twice my size
and front teeth with impeccable enamel.
Years ago, the opposite was true.
Toss it, it's useless.

And this dress was worn only once –
to a romantic dinner.
Another date like that
won't happen for a thousand years,
and by then, the dress will be out of fashion anyway.
Dump it, it's just taking up space.

This white cardigan is pure nostalgia for the past;
the blue one looks to the future.
They suck the oxygen out of the room at night.
Get rid of both of them!

This black corduroy jacket, cheap
threads from a second-hand store. Keep it!
It's always easier to hide behind someone else's skin.

This eccentric shirt with its black and white lines –
an alibi for finding yourself in two places at once.
Keep it! Too late to change your style!

This coat, heavy like inland fog,
two sizes too big, too expensive,
bought in a hurry for a ceremony,
hung only in hallways.
I'm still paying for it. Let it be!

These classic high-heel shoes
just have no instinct to return. Out they go!
Throw out these fine boots, too –
they only brought you bad luck from the start.
Sailors are right in saying,
'Don't put on new shoes when crossing unknown seas!'

And here are the grey clothes, my favourites, one after the other…
Without them, I'm exposed, like a drooling dog!
They're old, but must be kept!

And this scarf in bold colours
like a humid, crowded, and chaotic city
is a gift from someone who
wanted to get lost somewhere through me.
Throw it away! There's no space for it!

And this small purse that holds almost nothing:
a handkerchief, a phone number, a tube of foot cream.
Keep it, this spare alter ego –
it might come in handy one day.

And red… what's a red sweater doing in my drawer?
Looking for a fight?
Throw it out, what are you waiting for?

And finally, wrinkle-free, everyday
comfortable clothes that never disappoint.
A string of compromises that have taken the shape of my body.
Keep them for sure – you're not allowed to toss these!

On the floor, the discarded clothes evaporate, a gigantic
womb that held a woman's fantasies, now miscarried.
And the few items left
can finally move their elbows freely in the dresser
like gondoliers on a perfect strip of water.

But to this day I haven't understood
if my mother was complaining or making excuses
when she mumbled, 'It's pure wool, hand-made',
whenever she cleaned her only suit with a few drops of petrol.

Water and Carbon

1

Revelation came to you on a September day,
not on top of a barren mountain but in the chemistry lab
during the last class period when you were starving,
when, after Hamlet's monologue and equations with two unknowns,
it became clear there was nothing more to learn.

'Human beings are simply made of water and carbon,' he declared,
and drew a long formula with many holes on the chalkboard
that looked like a metal trap for rabbits.
He was the messenger, St John the Chemistry Teacher,
drenched in sweat, his belt buckled tight.
Face cleanly shaved, hair trimmed and parted flat with Figaro oil...

Wasn't he supposed to look a little more miserable?
Wasn't he supposed to have a long beard?
Wasn't a bush nearby supposed to have burst into flames?

'Simply water and carbon!
Maybe even a little magnesium, nitrogen, calcium, and phosphorus...
In short, little choice involved.'
And he chucked the chalk into the air
as if a key to a door without hinges.

He clasped his hands. Mission accomplished!
The last words already spoken.
Now disperse and spread the good news!
Or go to hell – who cares!

A bitter relief in the air, the scent of freshly cut grass.
Suddenly, we no longer knew who we were;
suddenly we were all the same.

So why the eternal worry on my mother's face?
And what sort of chemical compounds
were Adler and Schopenhauer talking about in the other classroom
from which only a thin wall separated us
or was it an entire existence?

2

Water and carbon. Measurable.
When you're born they measure your weight, your height and
     heartbeat;
they encase and stamp you with a belly button like a leaden seal
you have no authority to open! (You have no authority over
     yourself.)
They measure your temperature, in the shade of course,
your sugar levels, albumen, iron, reflexes on your knees,
your tongue, twice, before and after a meal.
(What does this have to do with speaking?!)

They measure the circumference of your head
to fit you with a hat so you can think with a cool brain,
and your chest for a suit, the tailor's
icy cold hands tickling your armpits and ribs,
and making you nervous.
They fill your clothes with padding
so no one can hear what's going on inside you.
Double-breasted, single-breasted, spare buttons, fake pockets on
     your pants.
All yours! Now you're one of us!
Welcome to the kingdom of water and carbon!

When they recruit you they give your naked body a check-up.
You have to be healthy, the impeccable lamb of the herd
for a sacrifice in the name of your country.
Give to Caesar what belongs to Caesar.

But you're unsure what to cover with your hands.
Between your genitals and shaved head
you choose your genitals
forgetting that the mane
is precisely what makes a lion king.

'To protect what? Where my territory begins and ends?'
Nothing is yours.
Attack and invade. Use trickery like the knight in a chess game:
two squares horizontally, one vertically.
Ambush your fate, face to face, or from behind,
when it least expects you.

And don't forget: as soon as you plant your feet somewhere,
hang a torn shirt or a pair of ragged pants outside on a clothes line,
enough to frighten the crows.
This is your passport –
poverty makes you a citizen anywhere you go;
poverty makes you indigenous.

3

Your body throws you under the bus; your body betrays you.
Your body is simply water and carbon.

I was 17 one morning in my prison cell
when after a night of delirium, running a 107-degree fever
caused by bronchopneumonia,
I woke up drenched in my own urine.
I was neither a child nor a man any more.

Then in the labour camp, out in the marsh,
I saw the theologian gathering rotten bits of cigarettes,
smelling the butts, trying to take a single drag.

But when I saw the former Sorbonne professor,
secretly digging through the trash and pick up a piece of water-
    melon rind,
which he then wiped on his pants and swallowed whole without
    chewing,
I knew I witnessed five thousand years of civilisation
extinguished in one moment.

Of course, it's always the fault of the witness,
the wrong eyes at the wrong place.
Without a witness we wouldn't even have crematoriums
and only white fumes would leak out of history's nostrils.

4

He had such dignity, the old man who hung himself
(rejected here on earth and now also in heaven),
his bare feet like a saint's, his body a frozen planet
revolving one last time around itself,
his head drooped to one side,
as if he were refusing to witness even his own death...

But it didn't end here; they plucked out his gold teeth
as if removing three generations of his history.
Declassed, disgraced, even among the dead.
How can a toothless man protect himself at the Last Judgement?
How could he formulate his arguments?
The dead would laugh; angels would shake their heads.

And so he too would be forgotten.
Simply water and carbon like everyone else.

The living went back to work, eyes cast down as if at their own
    funeral.
The whips against their joints and back
gave them no time to think much.

You can't be last in line – this was the goal,
morning to night.

But where was our country at that moment? Where was Caesar?

5

'They stripped us naked
and beat us under cold tap water
with Soviet boots. We fainted. But...'

'But?'

'But the next day all four of us were still alive at roll call.
And the officers made a bet for a case of beer on the boy from Tropoja
having left him outside in the snow all night long
naked as the day he was born.
But...'

'But?'

'But one of them lost the bet.'

'... ?'

'When they beat the old man like a child, slapping him in the face,
I did nothing to help him...'

'... ?'

'Then I knew that even death didn't give a damn about us. It
          approached us like a dog,
sniffed us then left us alone...'

'...'

'We were simply femur bones, without marrow.'

And his eyes suddenly beamed, as if he had just found
a nail on the wall where he could hang a painting:
'However, Sergeant Halim was a good man...'

'What good things did Sergeant Halim do?'

'He didn't do anything good,
but he didn't do anything bad either.'

6

Then one day you became one with suffering,
as it transformed into a limb
that must be treated generously like your other limbs:
wash it, clean it, cut its nails carefully, keep it warm,
feel its numbness
like when you placed your arm beneath your head late at night,
dumping all your sleepless weight onto it, and the searchlight
scanned the camp
moving cunningly across the brown blankets
like the eye of a jackal preying on the weakest animal in the herd.

Nothing and no one came between you and your suffering.
One dissolved into another like salt in water
(and now you can't remember which one of you preceded the other).

And you quit complaining.
From your lungs carbon streams out freely.

7

'I'm tired of listening to you. Enough now.
Tell me just one thing: Why did you tolerate all this?'

asks his brother from an ocean away
groomed by Hudson's breeze.
He lives in a country where the right to pursue happiness
is guaranteed by the constitution.

'And what should we have done according to you?'

'Some of you should have been killed,
so the rest could live with dignity.'

But this doesn't follow chemistry's laws.
The sole mission of water and carbon
is to stay alive at all costs.

And to stay alive they simply need their basic instincts,
as basic as the words and phrases in the small pocket dictionary
tourists carry in foreign lands.
Like for example: 'bread', 'water', 'How do you get to the nearest
    town?'
'Do you have a vacant room for tonight?' 'I can pay cash.'

Because of these instincts
some of us returned home alive
with a pair of borrowed shoes.
We built a hut of reeds and mud where we could begin again
under a sky where a colourless porridge cooked in a pot
with all the leftover seeds
like Noah's porridge.
We were guns without latches.
We softened walls with our shadows.
And we bore children, two-dimensional children,
like ribbons of light that enter through the crack of a door
or through the torn tarp on a roof.
Daydreaming children, the children of survival
who noticed only the bonny haunches of the farm oxen,

and at night, like a secret sect,
gathered around Dickens.

8

You can't conquer evil. Evil ends on its own.

No matter how great, every evil has its moment of saturation:
murderous sharks, wars, inquisition fires,
cholera and the plague, destructive glaciers too...
Even dictatorships reach their saturation point
when sulfur spills out of their sickened stomachs.

And blessed is the one destined to live through the Epoch of
    Saturation:
like paradise in those illustrated religious flyers
where tigers and humans bask peacefully together under the sun,
in an apple orchard by a river of honey, co-sufferers and co-citizens.

Fault is not a feature of water or carbon.
Fault doesn't exist.

9

Children, yes,
but adults never abandon their toys.

Among tin bowls and aluminium spoons,
coats and clogs of the same size, among shaved heads
we were identified by our lost causes:
one believed in 'the republic', one in 'the monarchy',
one in 'the revolution', one in 'the truth',
and one simply in 'health'.

(A little too much faith there in thirteen square feet of space.)

And the one who used to talk to himself or to a corner of the wall
once got a little carried away when he claimed to be Constantine
    the Great.
Mind separate from body,
he was more akin to the Constantine Colossus
with two right hands in the Palazzo dei Conservatori.

You have no right to occupy two places in this world;
even in prison there is no space for two selves.
So one day they took him away, all of his pieces,
to who knows where; whichever piece ended up in court
and whichever in the madhouse...
And he was only twenty-five years old.

Observed from above
we were simply part of a museum –
somewhere a millwheel shone, somewhere a parchment yellowed,
and somewhere else a horseman's costume hung
without a horseman in sight.

   10

Water is recyclable.
Nature is a good housewife and lets nothing go to waste.

They say the one who posed for Jesus' portrait in *The Last Supper*
was the same person who posed for Judas' four years later,
though this time not the soft-skinned, golden-haired choir boy
any more, but the man in a prison in Rome, convicted of serious
    crimes.

Water
can do wonders in four years –
it can freeze, turn cloudy or stale, flow out of its bed –
wonders that even Da Vinci's eagle eye
couldn't predict.

And so each of us could have four lives.
In the most fortunate case
we could be recycled from a balloon into cleaning gloves,
then into a car seat, and in the end into the synthetic snow
that falls on a romantic Christmas scene shoot in mid-July
until the director is satisfied and yells, 'Cut!'

Where there's hope, there's compromise.

But what can be said of the man
who willingly chose to die of starvation?
Ecce homo they shouted mockingly – people in uniform,
the materialists who couldn't wait to wash their hands.

Because dignity, if not inherited, can be contagious.

11

Water has a short memory.

From Palm Sunday to Good Friday there were five blessed days;
the one they welcomed as triumphant into Jerusalem
was nailed as 'faithless' on the fifth day.

'But, if we're only water and carbon,
then what is love? How do we know it's love?'

You can't know, but others can;
when they see you roofless, they think:
'There was a fire there!'

At the camp, when mail arrived on Tuesdays – letters from wives,
fiancées, lovers – one of us always ended up empty-handed;
'No letters for you!' meaning, 'She left you.'
In that moment all eyes seized you

and conjugated the verb 'to leave' into all the tenses, forms, persons
beyond etymologies, all the way to Salome
and the 'Dance of the Seven Veils'...
Never before did you feel so naked,
so naked that they could count the hairs and pores on your body,
the nerves firing under your skin like frantic moles.
They could easily make out your heart
a late tomato on the vine, unripe, green,
so green you were stunned.

From war and love,
you return even more ignorant
than when you first set out.

12

'You are free,' they told him after forty-five years.
'Where will you go now?'
They could've been asking someone on death row,
'What song do you want to hear?' Or more precisely,
'Do you know what you've lost?'
A second punishment, a second execution.

It was the end of June. The sky opened its mouth ear to ear
and laughed brazenly, exposing a cluster of clouds
above some lonely mountain peaks,
and the ticket seller her wisdom teeth
when he asked, 'A ticket to the sea, please!'

The journey was long,
the longest our kind of water and carbon could ever take,
in a boxcar that smelled of freshly baked buns and sweat.
He stopped at the wrong station.
Travelled the rest of the journey on foot.
The breeze from the poplars blew softly against his neck;

he felt like a newlywed entering the bedroom for the first time,
not knowing if that gesture was meant to be congratulatory or
        consoling.

And here's the sea!
How can man hide such a miracle from man?
How can you hide water from water?

Where had he seen that white ship leaving the dock before?
In the dreams of the father, grandfather, great-grandfather?
Around him circled men and women in speckled bathing suits
and joyous children with sunburned shoulders.
He was the only one in the wrong season –
late, premature.
He was the only one fully clothed, from head to toe,
as if a black piano shut in the corner of a hall
around which the world revolves undisturbed.

He touched the sand –
only a single grain finds its way into the belly of an oyster
with time and pain, to be transformed into a pearl.

Home Sweet Home

There's the house from which I stole eighteen years.
(To all the other houses I gave and gave.)
Over pierced with nails, scratched by cats,
wrinkled from soap, pampered by secrets told behind doors,
awakened by roosters, put to sleep by the gutters' grief,
and aged on Sundays, the only days people own.
(Then to whose account do all the others belong?)
When you have no hope at all,
you're free to point at any plane,
without appearing ridiculous:
'Our children will go to Harvard.'
But back then, if you pointed your finger at the closest town,
you were making a promise. Better not do it.

A house vanished at weddings and rediscovered at funerals.
New windows on top of old ones. Shades. Functional doors:
to enter, exit, or hang your hats.
An overloaded house like an envelope full of stamps and seals,
which, having gone around the world,
returns unopened to the sender
stamped with 'Wrong Address' in the corner.
With half of its body paralysed by darkness,
the house now waits to learn of its past through you.
Make something up if you've got nothing to say;
point your finger at any plane.
In the end, everyone's life
is only a question of narrative skill.

But at night,
water pipes buzz, beams crack up in laughter.
The dead whisper in the house's ear,

certainly some joke, or the truth
which reveals the naïve imagination we possess,
just about useless.

This Gesture

Look what we have here:
some books bought with a little savings,
as if land purchased for a house
that you might never build. Plato, Hegel, *The Marxist Movement*,
heavy cloth covers. Sideways, behind Aristotle, rests Art Nouveau,
like the head of a woman nodding off on the train,
your shoulder still out of politeness.
Books in foreign languages, bought with the last change
from shops you'll never visit again:
Tarkovsky's Techniques, exchanged for five food vouchers;
Bergman, Hitchcock, Louis Buñuel reveal only part of the wall,
each the end of a misleading path inside a pyramid.
African Masks, Aztec Culture, Egyptian Gods
all bought on a rainy day perhaps, as an excuse to stay indoors.
And again the visual arts albums
labelled *Ars* in Latin like medicinal bottles
that camouflage a bitter taste.

Hugo, Turgenev, Stendhal...
relics of first love, second love, of...
A dark empty space
and further, Dostoyevsky's *White Nights*
with its green irony on the cover that says,
'Throw a coat over your shoulders first...'

And lower, Gaudí and other architectural books...
A smooth transition between what you wanted
and what you were able to attain.
Encyclopaedias, temples without roofs.
Shakespeare exchanged for a noisy Soviet radio.

Poetry books: thin, sly, bought at discounted prices,
breaking apart like crumbled bread thrown at swans in the park.

The only ones arranged horizontally
are *The Erotic Art of the Middle Ages*, *The Ethical Slut*, and *Tropic
    of Cancer* –
easy to find when feeling around in the dark,
like slippers under the bed.

In a corner, the holy books, the Gospels.
They've arrived here by themselves – you didn't spend a cent to
    buy them.
Each volume almost never opened. How can you believe
    something
that doesn't ask for anything in exchange?

And on the very bottom, *The Barbarian Invasion*, history, science…
Time to read with glasses. Linear reading. Andropause.

To show someone your library is an intimate gesture,
like giving him a map, a tourist map of the self
marked with the museums, parks, bridges, galleries, hotels, churches,
    subway…
and the graveyards that appear regularly
at the edges of every town, at the beginning of every epoch.

The Stairs

My father was obsessed with stairs.
All his life he'd build one set and destroy another,
sometimes indoors, sometimes outdoors,
never finding the perfect way to go up.

I feel the same way.

There's a different view from above: streets
become tight ropes; gardens hide behind houses
like bite marks on a lover's neck; cosmic dust conceals
the rotation of pedestrians around a star and themselves.
Whereas the railroad track with its yellow and black lines
isn't the rattlesnake that makes your skin crawl...

Whenever I chose the quick stairs of the elevator,
I got stuck between floors, an irrational number.
What happened next not worth mentioning.

And then the escalators
that deliver you
intact
like a postal package to another era
without knowing what's inside you. You don't know either.

Poetry, too, is a way of moving up,
temptation through denial, *via negativa*,
but the room on the second floor stays damp and cold, vacant.

My aunt shows a scar on her knee
from her youth, caused by a nail on a wooden staircase –
she tells the same story over and over again.

I never understood what she was looking for,
those summer evenings on the roof,
but I imagine the sad creaking on the stairs, her solemn descent,
her cadence, like all other cadences, without nails, without wounds.

Lost in Translation

Dusk. The moon glides over abandoned houses
that stir like sleeping babies. Smoke still puffs out of
three or four chimneys. A dog's unanswered bark.
A gate closes. The light on the porch flickers from a sneeze.
Behind windows
you can see the shadows of a few people stuck between two epochs
like words lost in translation.

The closest school is now two hours away.
The church even farther;
it's useless to burn incense for just twenty souls.
Those who have left never return.
They only send letters slippery like butter.
They say they're doing fine.
Maybe they work on a farm there, too.
And anyway,
it's easier to blame a foreign land.

Autumn retreats
like a satisfied wolf;
she hides half of her prey under the first snow
certain that she'll find it untouched when she returns next year.
'Loneliness' you could call it.
But you need a second person to confirm this with a nod,
and the nearest barber is four hours away.

When he sees a crow fly away alone,
he whispers simply to his wife
back turned to her: 'Winter will be harsh.'

Nothing to blame here.
You can't find a more suitable landscape than this

to hang in the corridor
or inside a tired heart,
smack in the middle of blue, red, grey, ochre
or even white lime-washed walls.

A Perfect Day

This probably happens somewhere in Provence, doesn't it?
You wake up late, not in a hurry,
you open your window, and the heavy smell of earth
sprinkled with red poppy seeds floods in.
It could be May, and the cherries are in bloom.
The phone rings. It's your father,
letting you know that he's well and misses you.
(What's wrong? You've never heard those words from his mouth?
Weren't they so much like fruit without a pit?)
Then a warm bath to admire your body
as if in a Renaissance oil painting by François Clouet.
You go back to work in the studio – write nothing
or simply jot down some words. A single word would be ideal.
A single word, a need,
that puts your whole body into action, hands and feet,
like an old Singer sewing-machine.
Buzz, buzz. A bumblebee's nest in the garden. Nothing to worry
    about.
For lunch coq au vin accompanied by a glass of Minervois,
just before the uproar of children released from school.
In the evening, the love of your life takes you out to a terrace café
to show you how the sun sets,
its delicate exit, never turning its back,
like a baritone at the end of the show.
You happily talk to each other.
You wonder how much of the present is still unexploited:
'Such good wine!' 'You look so lovely in that dress!'
'How many years do you think that old couple has been together?'
Then you get a little carried away with the wine...
You've got only twenty four hours; no reason to feel guilty.
Then what? What happens next? I don't even know
and God damn it, the days are so long in May.

Perfect, yes.
But something makes you uneasy,
embarrassed, predictable,
like a winner's speech in your pocket:
what everyone knows you have
even though you may never use it.

One's Destiny

To this day
she keeps her dead sister's identity papers, still active,
her official name, date of birth, ID number.
Everything went wrong and nothing could've been different.
It was the other one's destiny
she slowly grew used to
as if a hotel room:
'What beautiful wallpaper!'
'What sad slippers on the carpet!'

Nothing was hers – this place simply temporary.
That's why she added no furniture and didn't plant anything on
        the balcony.
Letters that arrived to her door
were left unopened, tied together with string.

But someone else's destiny has a perfect pitch.
You can hear what's inside your head
as if sitting in a Greek amphitheatre
where in a few hours, a cheerful mother
will transform into Medea.

Now that her end is coming and she's ready to return the keys,
something hurts in her chest:
How could she not open one of those letters?
How could she not leave a single ironing mark on the bed sheet?

But at least she has her own alibi for her absence.
What is your excuse?

Inside a Suitcase

The first time I travelled by bus
it was June. Torrents of rain and vomit
streamed across the window,
fastening the landscape to my mind
with paper-clips.

Inside the wooden suitcase
between my knees, a few things rattled
as they slid from one side to the other.
There was no bigger shame –
the whole world knew what I was carrying.

I took that same journey many times.
In fact, it went even farther,
my own skin turning into a suitcase,
packed full with things, as if relocating to another life:
cotton things, synthetic things, truths, alibis, objects and shadows,
without the terror of the rattling emptiness.

If I try to remove certain things to get below the weight limit,
my skin thins, droops, and withers,
as if due to an extreme diet.

And after each return,
unused things fill other spaces
in my shelves, drawers, and imagination...

Only a few of them remain under my skin all year long.

But where can the knees of that nine-year-old be found?
Where are the brave sphinxes who protected
that suitcase, that small little empire of wood?

Things I Liked About Him

The way he approached the bed that first time,
somewhat tired, without turning to look outside
at the July afternoon full of cotton traps.
The way he switched off the light with a single touch
and unfolded the sheet with such certainty
as if he'd done it for a thousand years.

Like a large ship returning to port
with its last cargo; ready for the scrap.
It didn't matter any more what it stored inside –
bags of coffee, porcelain, or tropical fever.

TRANSLATOR'S ACKNOWLEDGEMENTS

Two dear mentors, Rosanna Warren and David Gullette, have helped me through the years by reading portions of these translations and noting corrections of idiomatic expressions. To Rosanna, for first steering me towards literary translation – a process of textual excavation, deep play, and continuing faith – and to David, for continuously nudging me to see better. I am deeply grateful for their friendship.

To Banff International Literary Translation Center and to OMI International Arts Center, for allowing me time and space to work on this book from start to finish.

To the NEA and English PEN, for their financial support.

To my parents, for unwavering faith in all my endeavours.

To Jeffrey Yang and Neil Astley, for their patience, kindness, and astute final edits of this book. Your help has been invaluable and I deeply admire your linguistic and poetic expertise.

To Mieke Chew at New Directions, for working like *a noiseless patient spider* answering all my e-mails in the final stages of this book.

To Luljeta, for trusting me to engage deeply with her poetry and for the generosity and freedom she gave me to create and recreate these poems. Everything I have learned about translation comes from my experience with her words.

To Albania, where I first discovered my love for words and language.

To my numerous translator friends and the entire 2015 BILTC family – your labours of love inspire me daily and I treasure you all.

And to the editors of the following publications in which some of these translations first appeared, sometimes in different forms: *AGNI Online, Ploughshares, World Literature Today, Two Lines, Seedings, Pangyrus Magazine, Asymptote Journal, Tupelo Quarterly, The Plume Anthology of Poetry 3 & 4, Catamaran Literary Reader, Liberation Poetry Anthology, Taos Journal of International Poetry and Art, PLUME*, and *3:AM Magazine*.

Thanks also to Matt O'Donnell at *From the Fishouse* for sharing some of these translations and an interview with Luljeta Lleshanaku in their audio archive (www.fishousepoems.org).

Ani Gjika is an Albanian-born poet, literary translator and writer. Her poetry book *Bread on Running Waters* (Fenway Press, 2013) was a finalist for the 2011 Anthony Hecht Poetry Prize and the 2011 May Sarton New Hampshire Book Prize. Gjika moved to the US when she was 18, earning an MA in English at Simmons College and an MFA in poetry at Boston University. She is the translator of Kosovar poet Xhevdet Bajraj's monodrama *Slaying the Mosquito* (Laertes Books, 2017) and her translation from the Albanian of *Negative Space* by Luljeta Lleshanaku was published by Bloodaxe in the UK and New Directions in the US in 2018. Her honours include awards and fellowships from the National Endowment for the Arts, the Robert Pinsky Global Fellowship, English PEN Translates, Framingham State University's Miriam Levine Award, and the Robert Fitzgerald Translation Prize.